FOSSILS UNCOVERED!

TINY GIANTS

TITANOSAUR DISCOVERY

By Sarah Eason
Illustrated by Diego Vaisberg

BEARPORT
PUBLISHING

Minneapolis, Minnesota

BEAR CLAW

Credits: 20b, © Marco Rubino/Shutterstock; 21t, © Veronika Surovtseva/Shutterstock; 21b, © Karkemish/Wikimedia Commons; 22l, © Kriengsak Wiriyakrieng/Shutterstock; 22r, © Microgen/Shutterstock; 23b, © LegART/Shutterstock.

Editor: Jennifer Sanderson
Proofreader: Harriet McGregor
Designer: Paul Myerscough
Picture Researcher: Rachel Blount

DISCLAIMER: This graphic story is a dramatization based on true events. It is intended to give the reader a sense of the narrative rather than a presentation of actual details as they occurred.

Library of Congress Cataloging-in-Publication Data

Names: Eason, Sarah, author. | Vaisberg, Diego, 1981- illustrator.
Title: Tiny giants : titanosaur discovery / by Sarah Eason ; illustrated by Diego Vaisberg.
Description: Bear claw books. | Minneapolis, Minnesota : Bearport Publishing Company, [2022] | Series: Fossils uncovered! | Includes index.
Identifiers: LCCN 2021026694 (print) | LCCN 2021026695 (ebook) | ISBN 9781636913377 (library binding) | ISBN 9781636913445 (paperback) | ISBN 9781636913513 (ebook)
Subjects: LCSH: Chiappe, Luis M.--Juvenile literature. | Titanosaurus--Patagonia (Argentina and Chile)--Juvenile literature. | Titanosaurus--Patagonia (Argentina and Chile)--Comic books, strips, etc. | Paleontological excavations--Patagonia (Argentina and Chile)--Juvenile literature. | Paleontology--Juvenile literature. | Badlands--Patagonia (Argentina and Chile)--Juvenile literature.
Classification: LCC QE862.S3 E276 2022 (print) | LCC QE862.S3 (ebook) | DDC 567.913--dc23
LC record available at https://lccn.loc.gov/2021026694
LC ebook record available at https://lccn.loc.gov/2021026695

For more information, write to Bearport Publishing, 5357 Penn Avenue South, Minneapolis, MN 55419. Printed in the United States of America.

CONTENTS

CHAPTER 1

A PUZZLE IN PATAGONIA

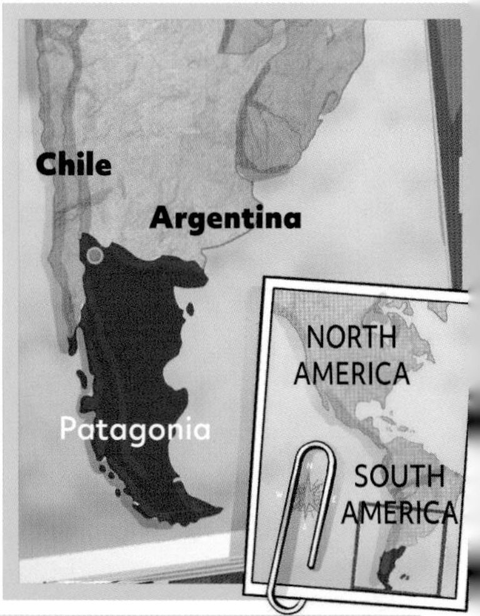

Chile
Argentina
Patagonia
NORTH AMERICA
SOUTH AMERICA

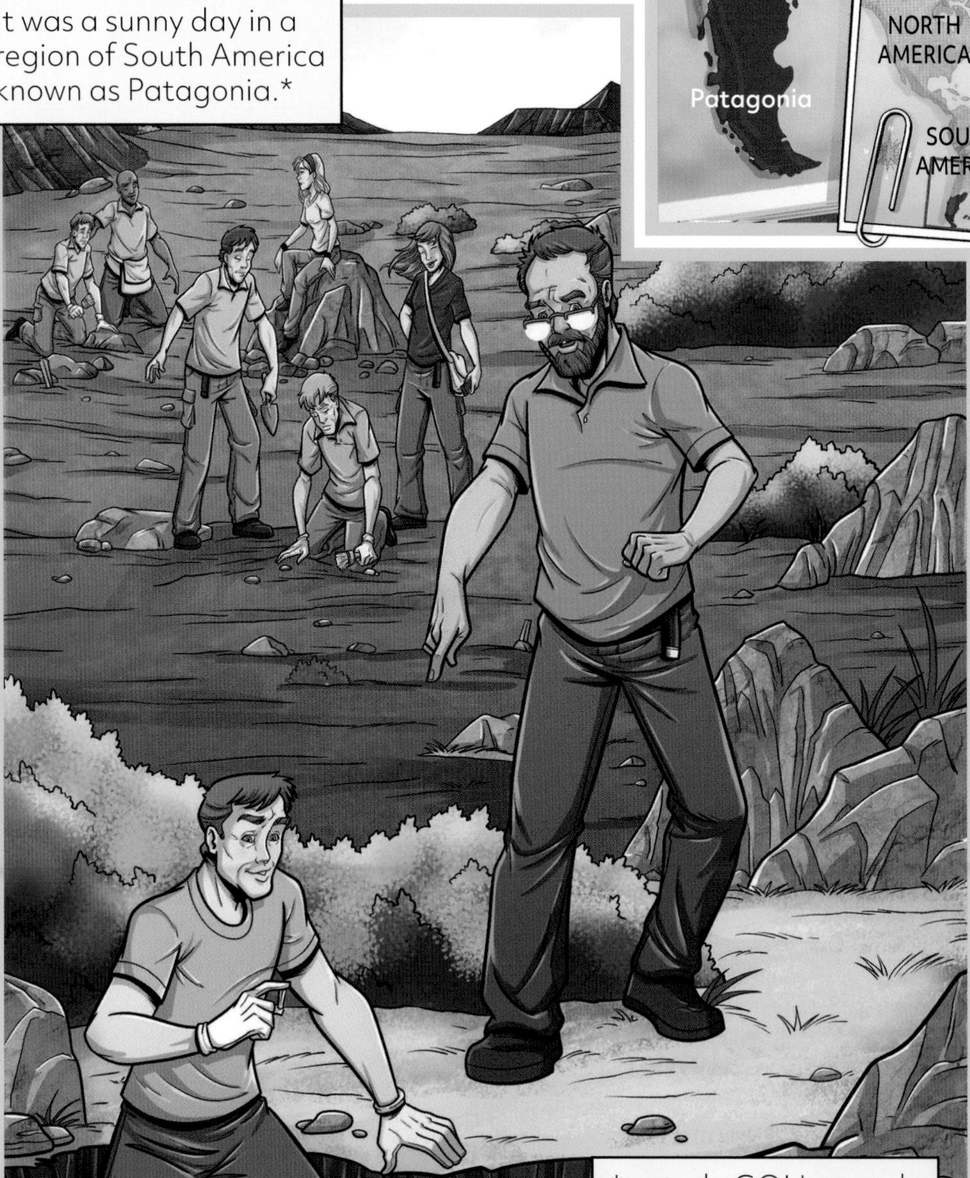

It was a sunny day in a region of South America known as Patagonia.*
*pat-uh-GOH-nee-uh

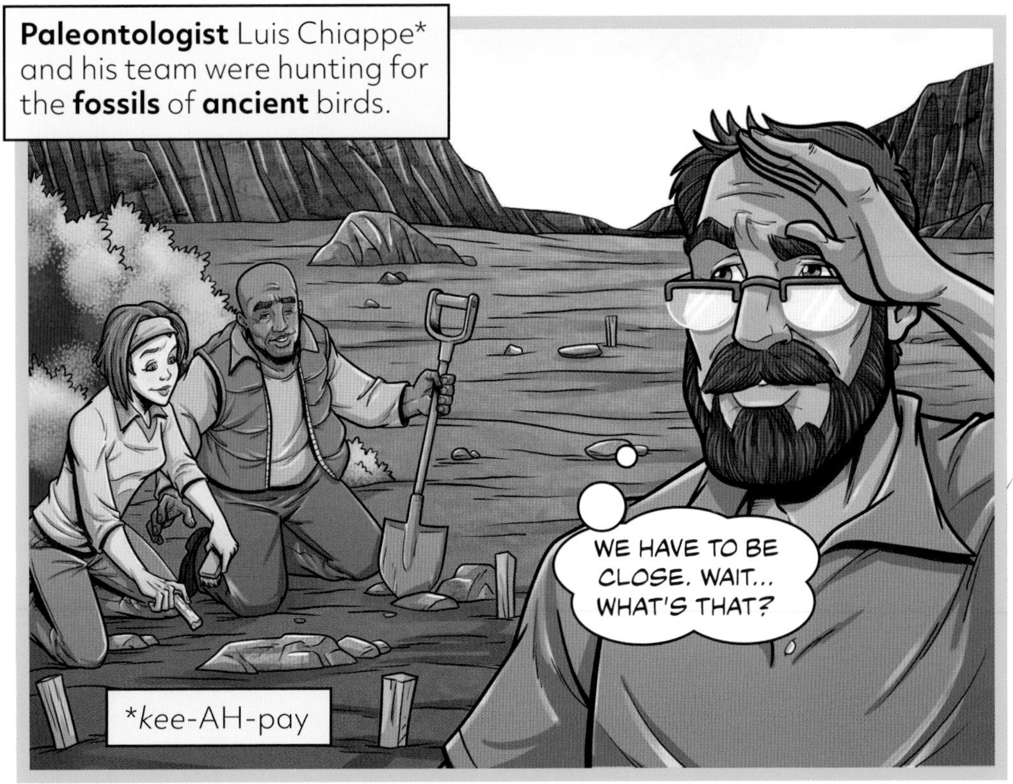
Paleontologist Luis Chiappe* and his team were hunting for the **fossils** of **ancient** birds.
WE HAVE TO BE CLOSE. WAIT... WHAT'S THAT?
*kee-AH-pay

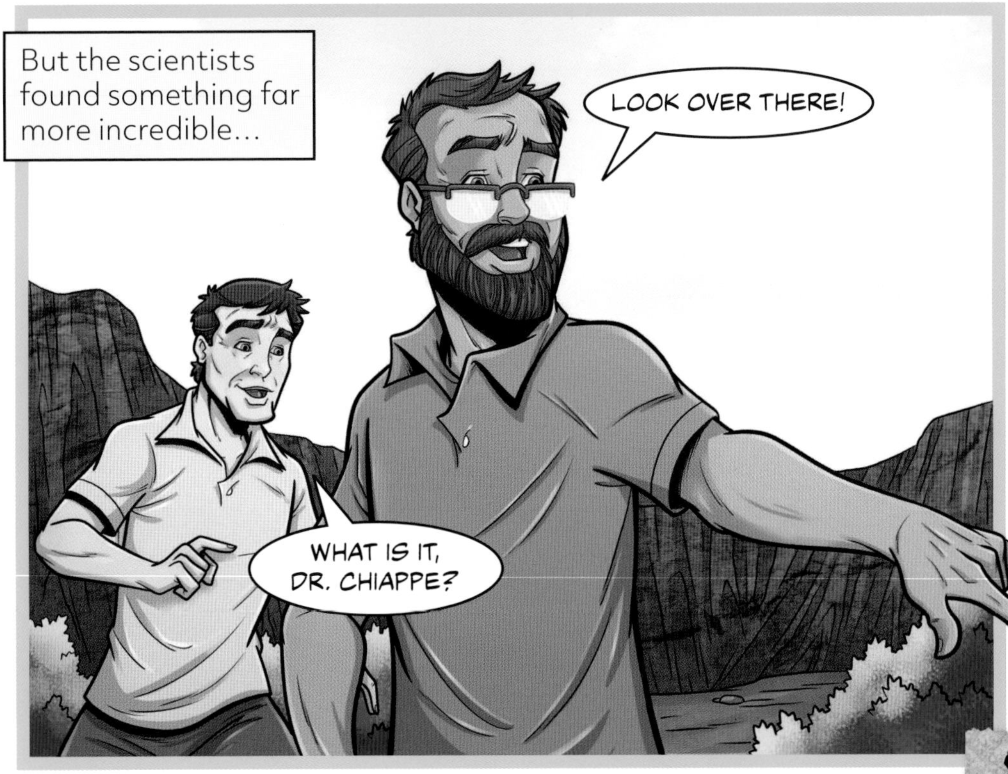
But the scientists found something far more incredible...
LOOK OVER THERE!
WHAT IS IT, DR. CHIAPPE?

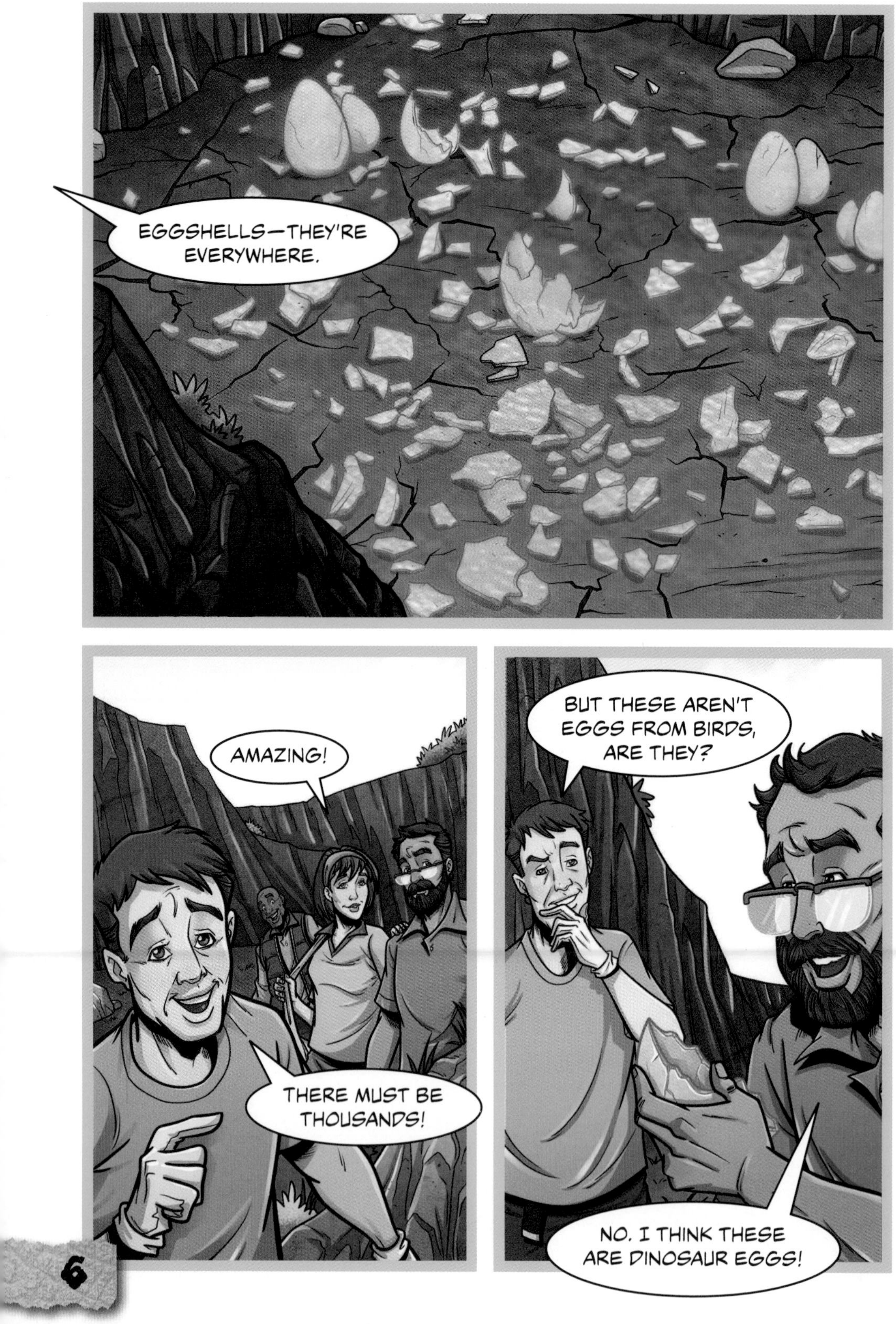
EGGSHELLS—THEY'RE EVERYWHERE.
AMAZING!
THERE MUST BE THOUSANDS!
BUT THESE AREN'T EGGS FROM BIRDS, ARE THEY?
NO. I THINK THESE ARE DINOSAUR EGGS!

It was an amazing discovery. Luis and the team had come upon the largest dinosaur **nesting site** ever found. Shells with rough, bumpy surfaces littered the ground. There were even some large, unbroken eggs.

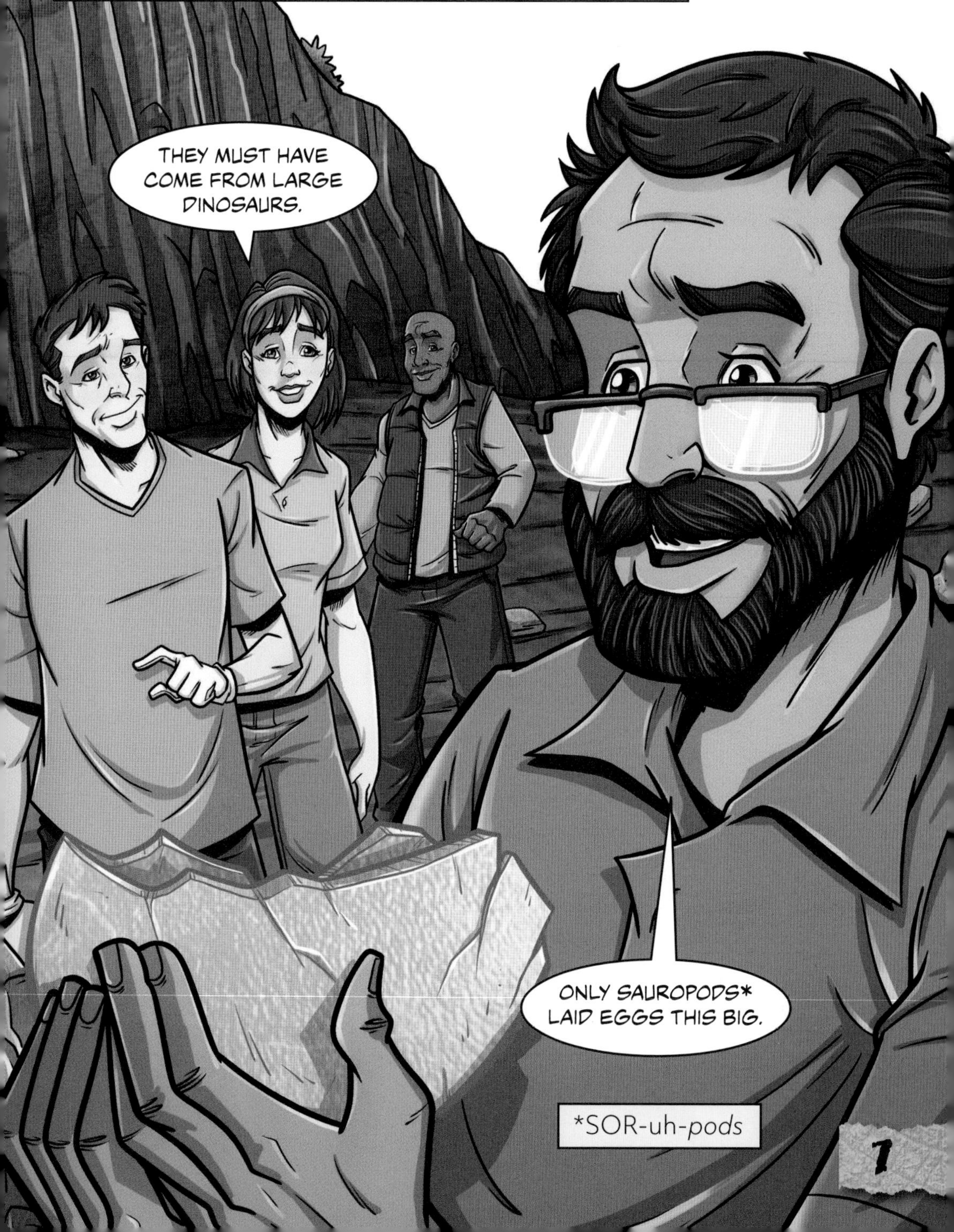

THEY MUST HAVE COME FROM LARGE DINOSAURS.
ONLY SAUROPODS* LAID EGGS THIS BIG.

*SOR-uh-*pods*

CHAPTER 2

ALL-TIME GIANTS

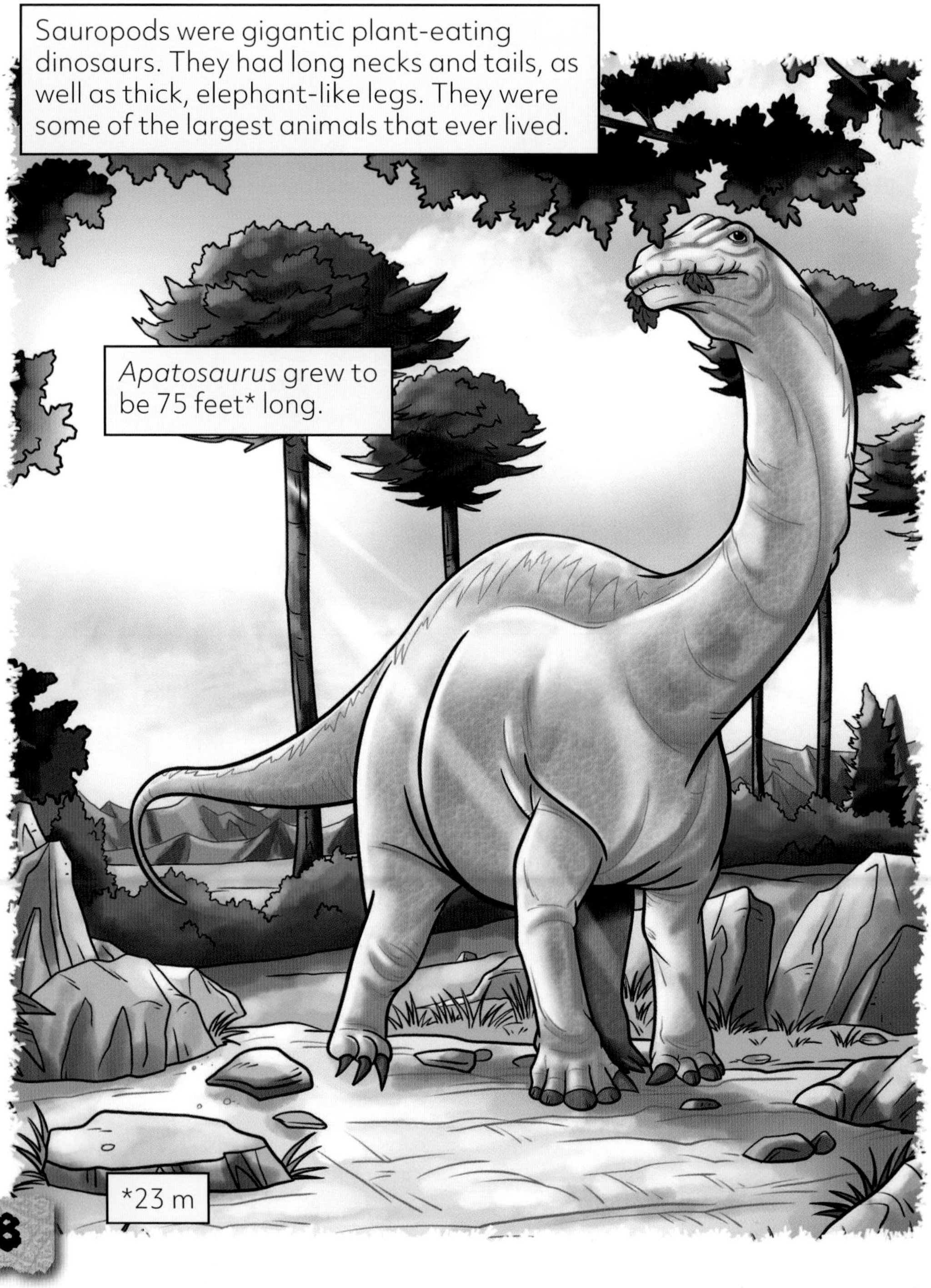
Sauropods were gigantic plant-eating dinosaurs. They had long necks and tails, as well as thick, elephant-like legs. They were some of the largest animals that ever lived.
Apatosaurus grew to be 75 feet* long.
*23 m

Diplodocus was even bigger. These sauropods could be up to 100 ft* in length.

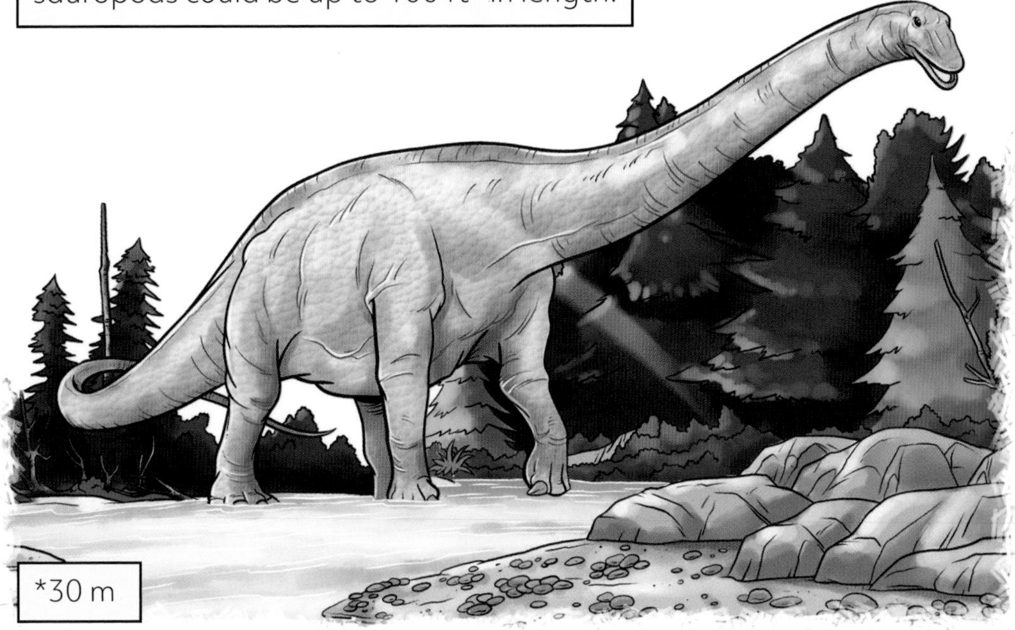

*30 m

Argentinosaurus is the largest dinosaur ever discovered. At up to 130 ft* long, it belonged to a group called titanosaurs. Luis thought his team had found eggs from these giants in Patagonia.

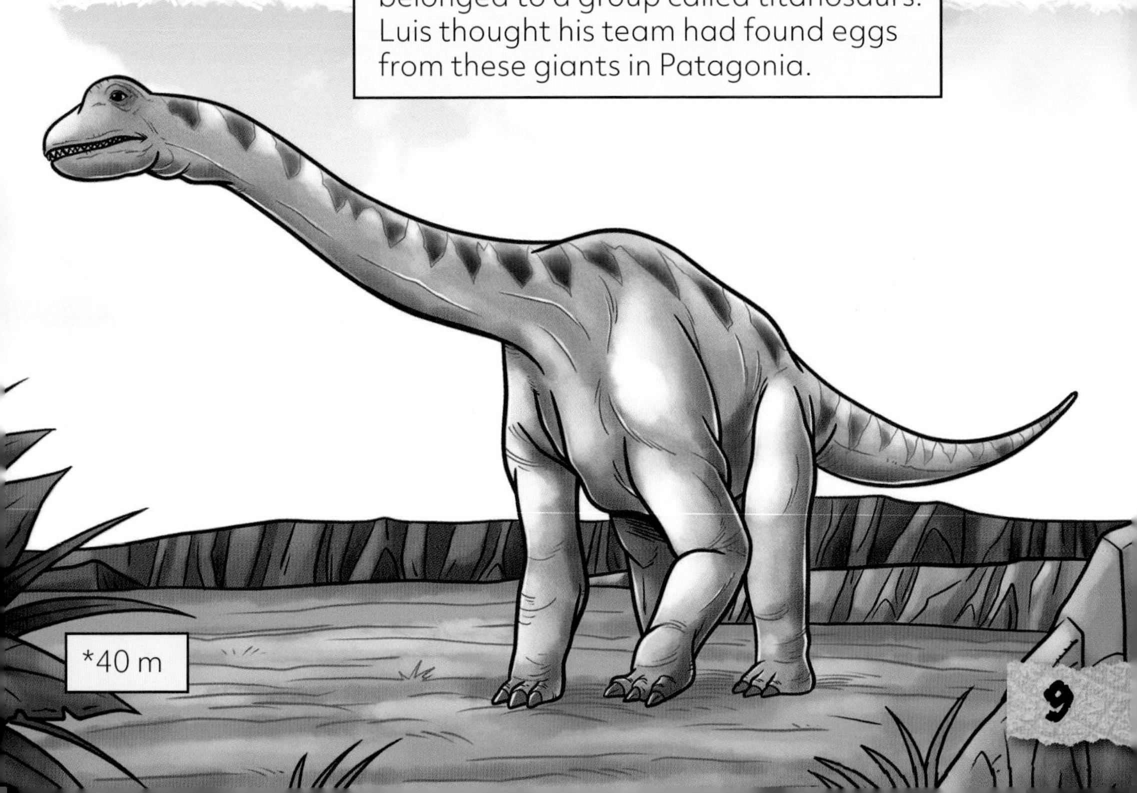

*40 m

But Luis needed more **evidence** to be sure he had the right dinosaur.

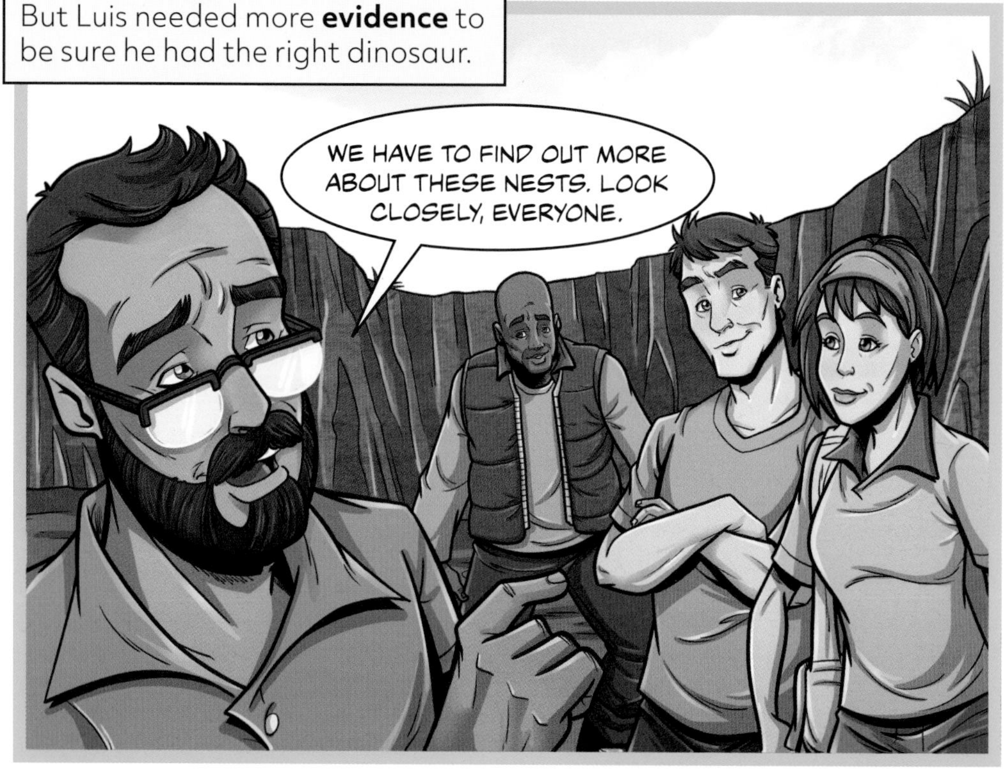
WE HAVE TO FIND OUT MORE ABOUT THESE NESTS. LOOK CLOSELY, EVERYONE.

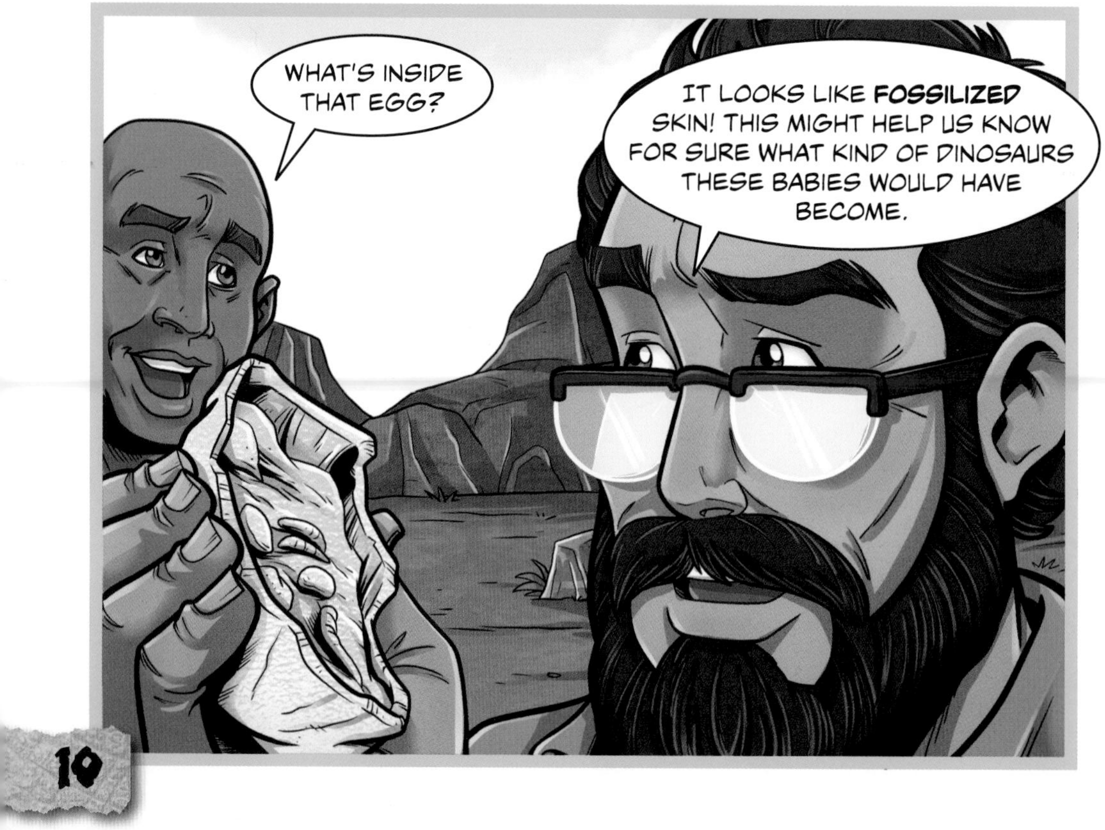
WHAT'S INSIDE THAT EGG?
IT LOOKS LIKE **FOSSILIZED** SKIN! THIS MIGHT HELP US KNOW FOR SURE WHAT KIND OF DINOSAURS THESE BABIES WOULD HAVE BECOME.

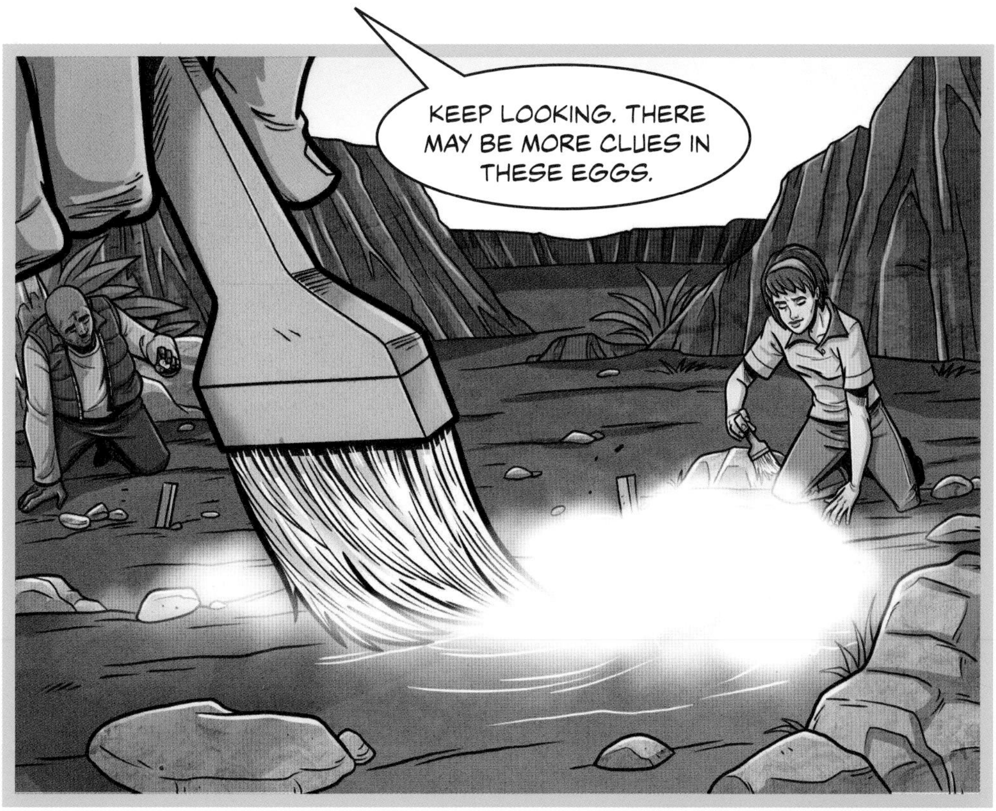
KEEP LOOKING. THERE MAY BE MORE CLUES IN THESE EGGS.

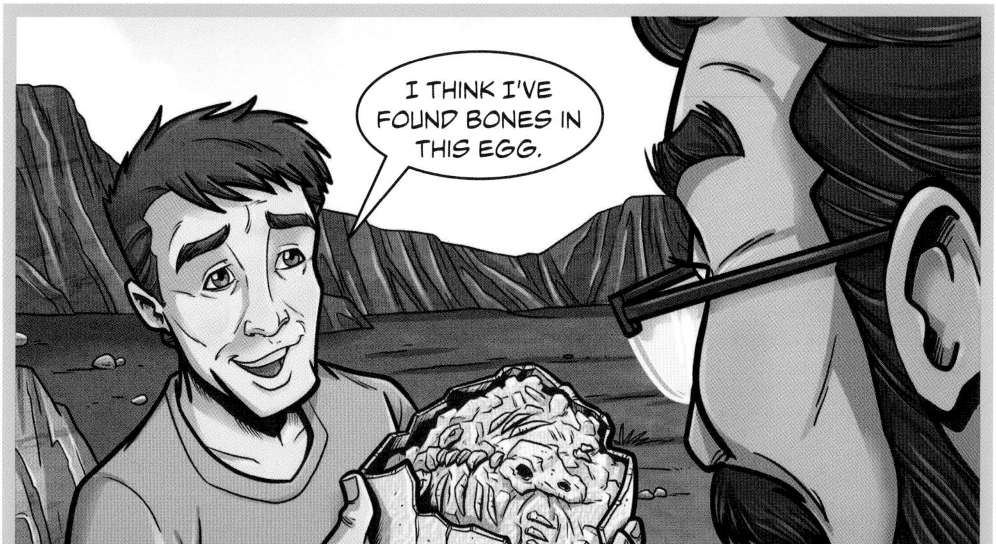
I THINK I'VE FOUND BONES IN THIS EGG.
GOOD WORK!

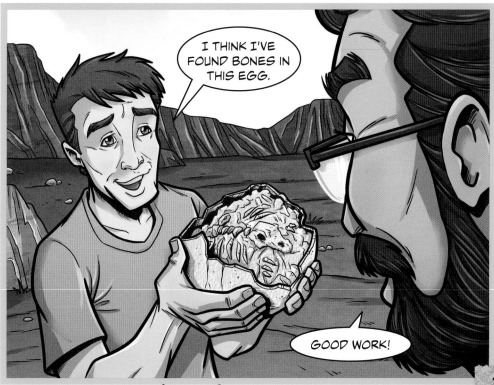

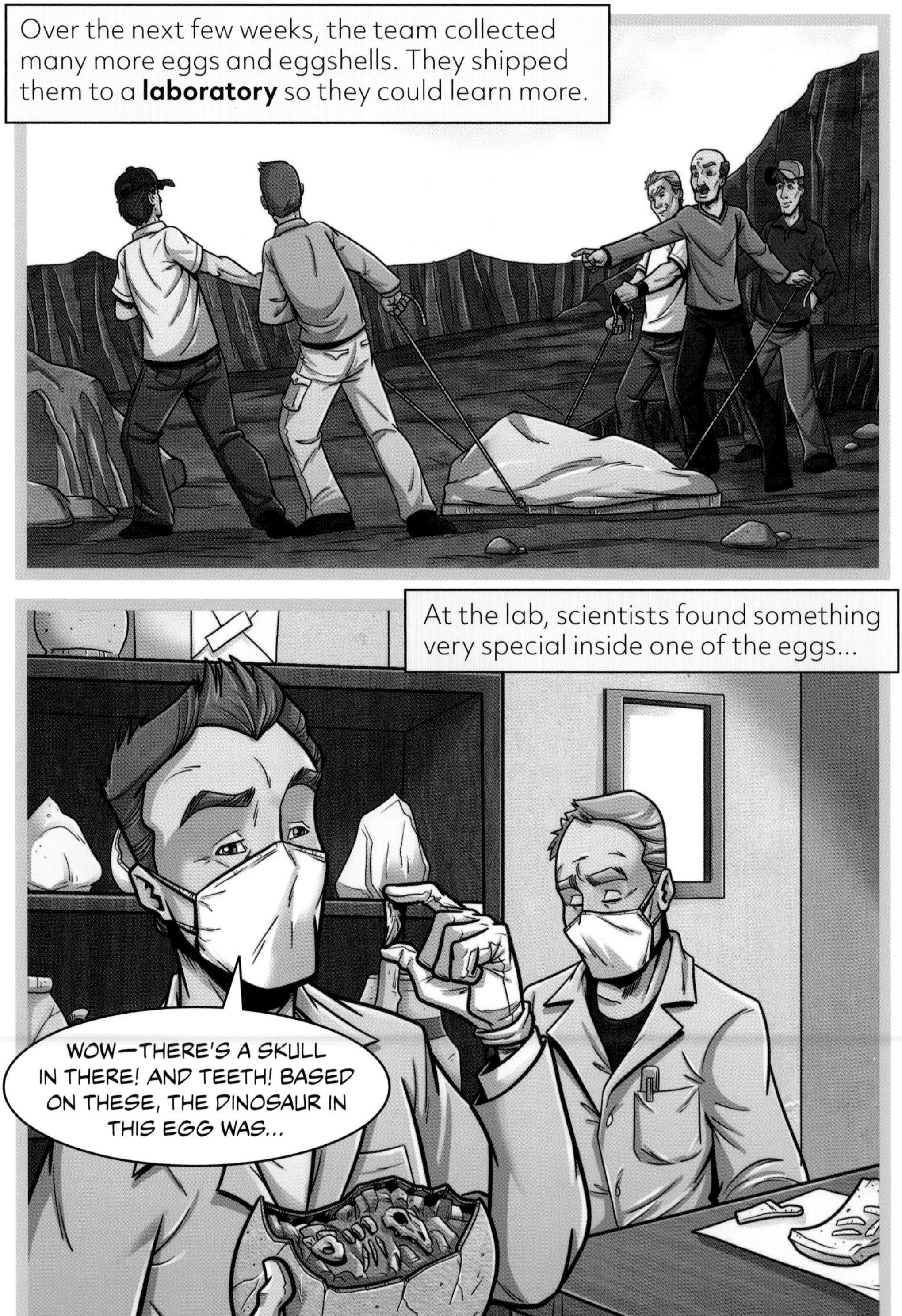
Over the next few weeks, the team collected many more eggs and eggshells. They shipped them to a **laboratory** so they could learn more.
At the lab, scientists found something very special inside one of the eggs...
WOW—THERE'S A SKULL IN THERE! AND TEETH! BASED ON THESE, THE DINOSAUR IN THIS EGG WAS...

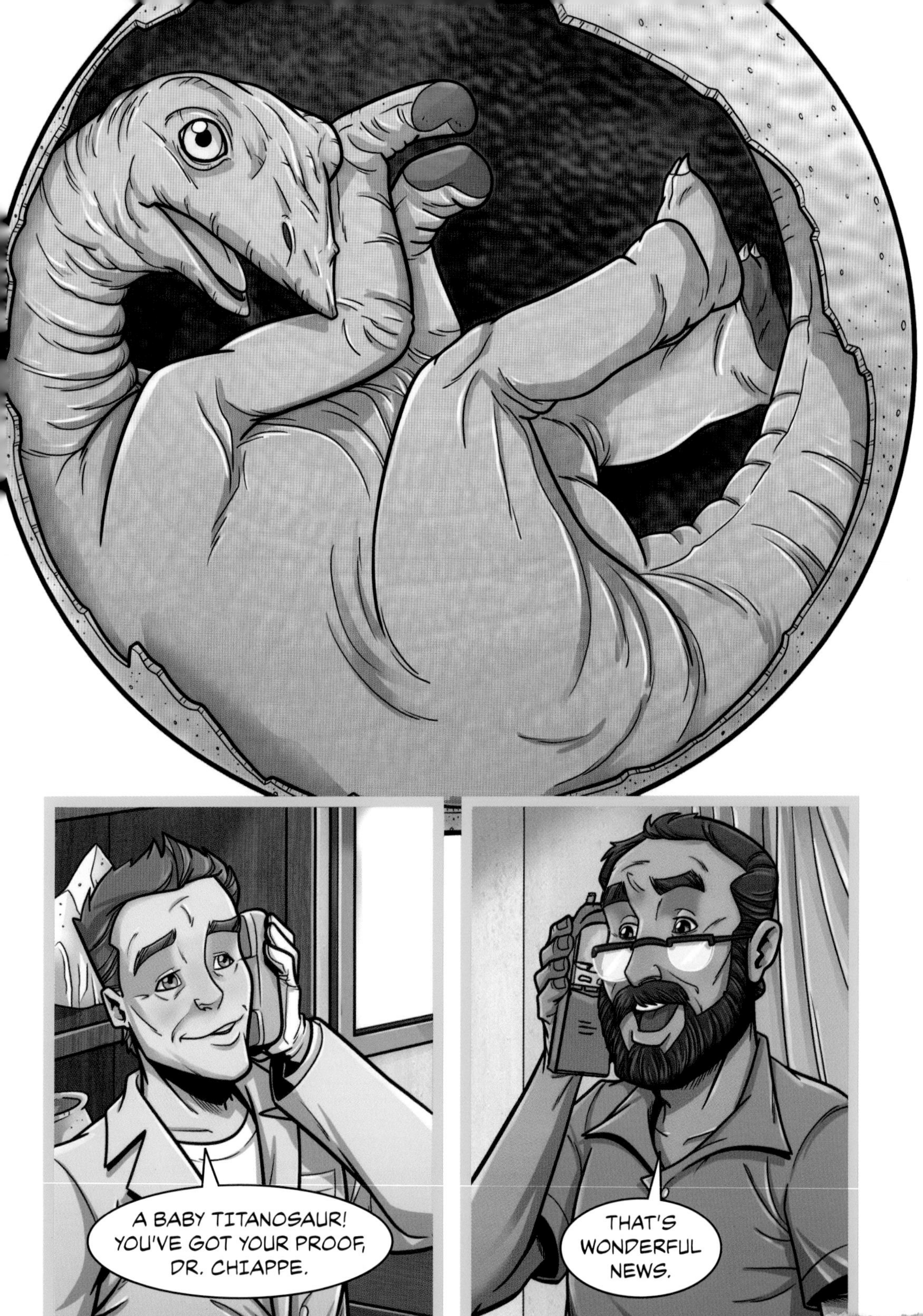
A BABY TITANOSAUR! YOU'VE GOT YOUR PROOF, DR. CHIAPPE.
THAT'S WONDERFUL NEWS.

CHAPTER 3

PUZZLE SOLVED

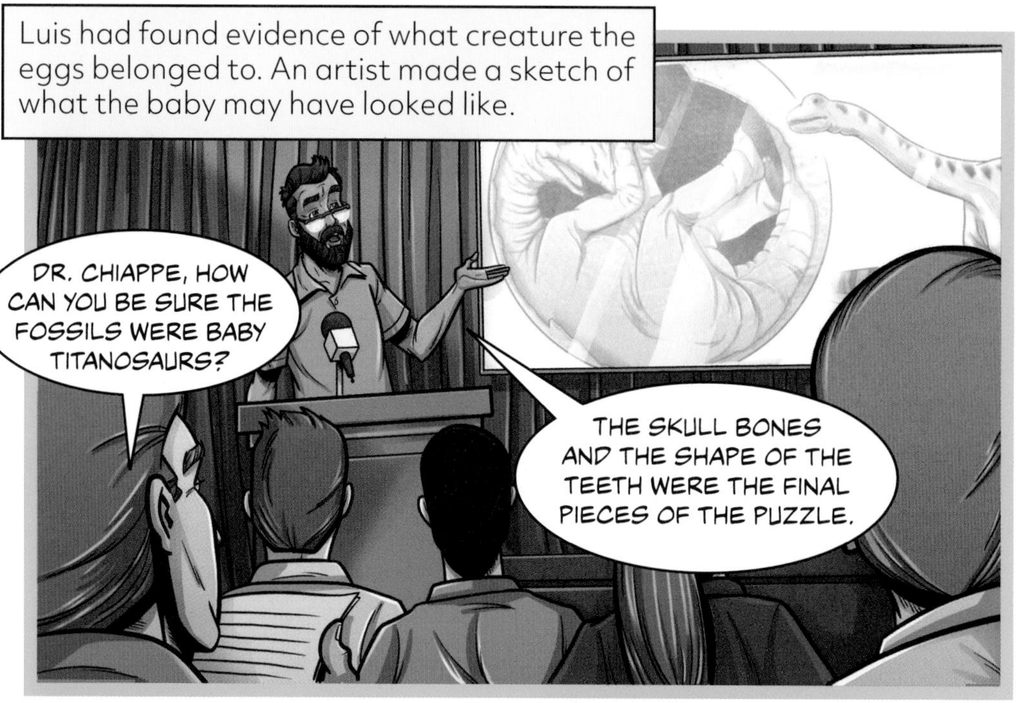
Luis had found evidence of what creature the eggs belonged to. An artist made a sketch of what the baby may have looked like.
DR. CHIAPPE, HOW CAN YOU BE SURE THE FOSSILS WERE BABY TITANOSAURS?
THE SKULL BONES AND THE SHAPE OF THE TEETH WERE THE FINAL PIECES OF THE PUZZLE.

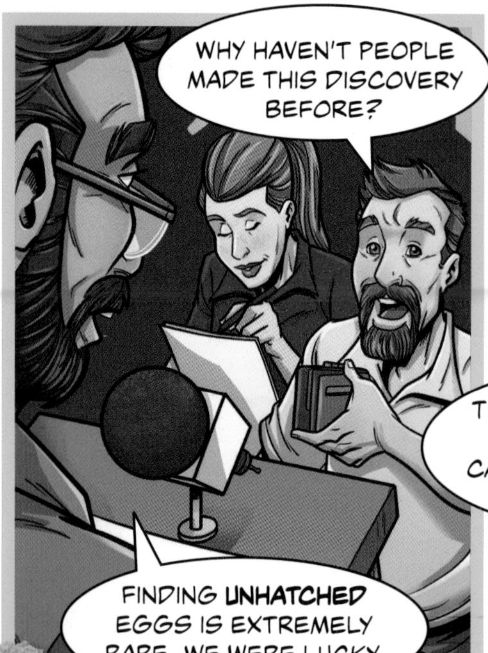
WHY HAVEN'T PEOPLE MADE THIS DISCOVERY BEFORE?
FINDING **UNHATCHED** EGGS IS EXTREMELY RARE. WE WERE LUCKY.

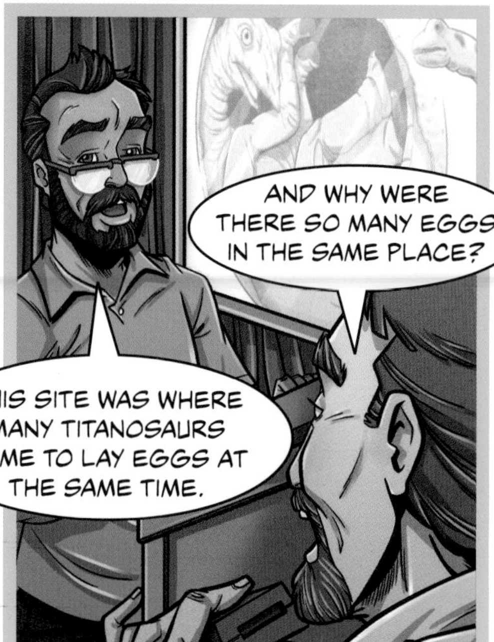
AND WHY WERE THERE SO MANY EGGS IN THE SAME PLACE?
THIS SITE WAS WHERE MANY TITANOSAURS CAME TO LAY EGGS AT THE SAME TIME.

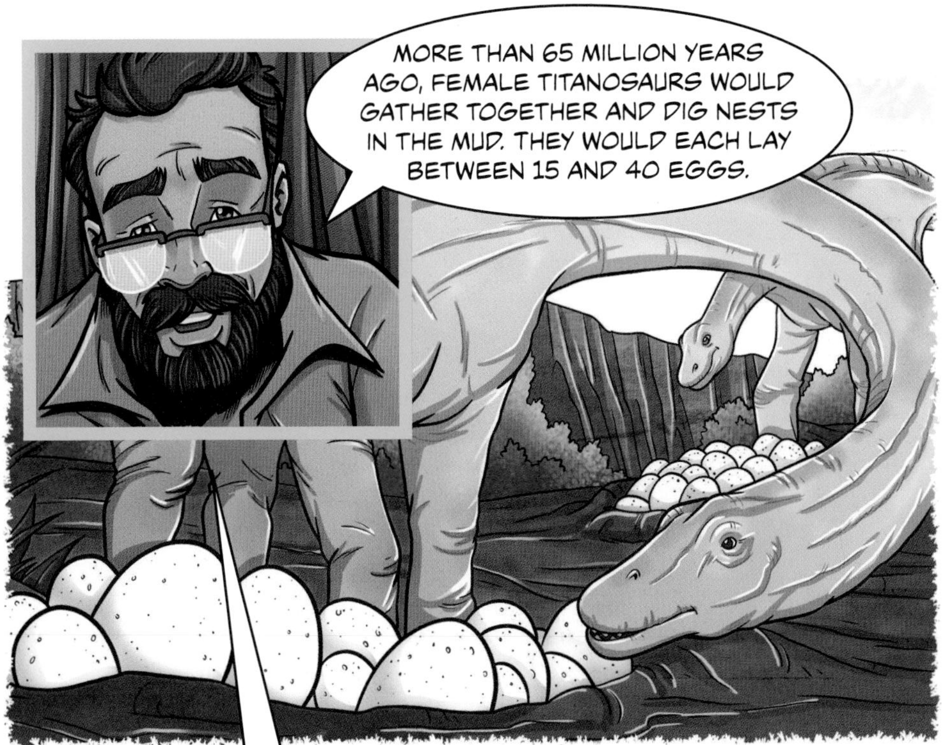

MORE THAN 65 MILLION YEARS AGO, FEMALE TITANOSAURS WOULD GATHER TOGETHER AND DIG NESTS IN THE MUD. THEY WOULD EACH LAY BETWEEN 15 AND 40 EGGS.

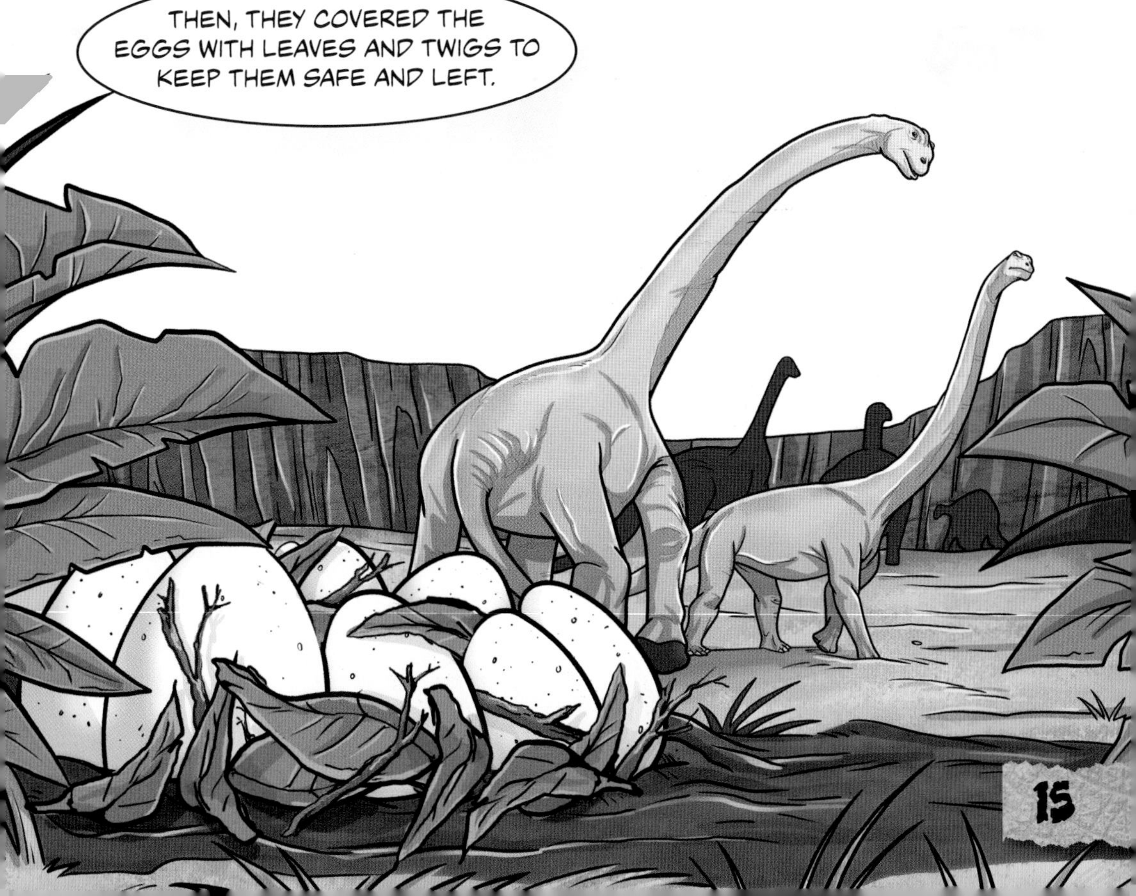

THEN, THEY COVERED THE EGGS WITH LEAVES AND TWIGS TO KEEP THEM SAFE AND LEFT.

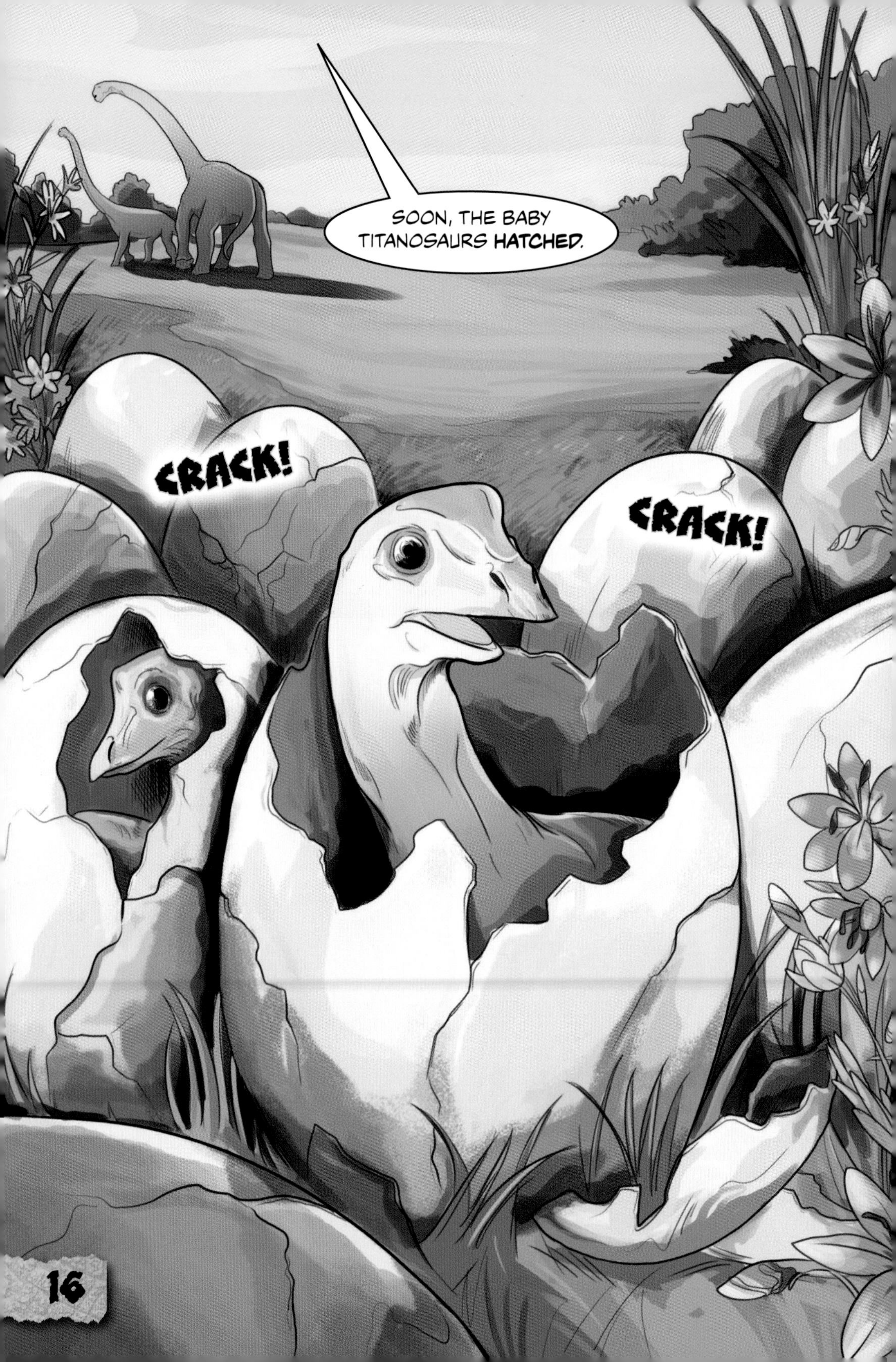
SOON, THE BABY TITANOSAURS **HATCHED**.
CRACK!
CRACK!

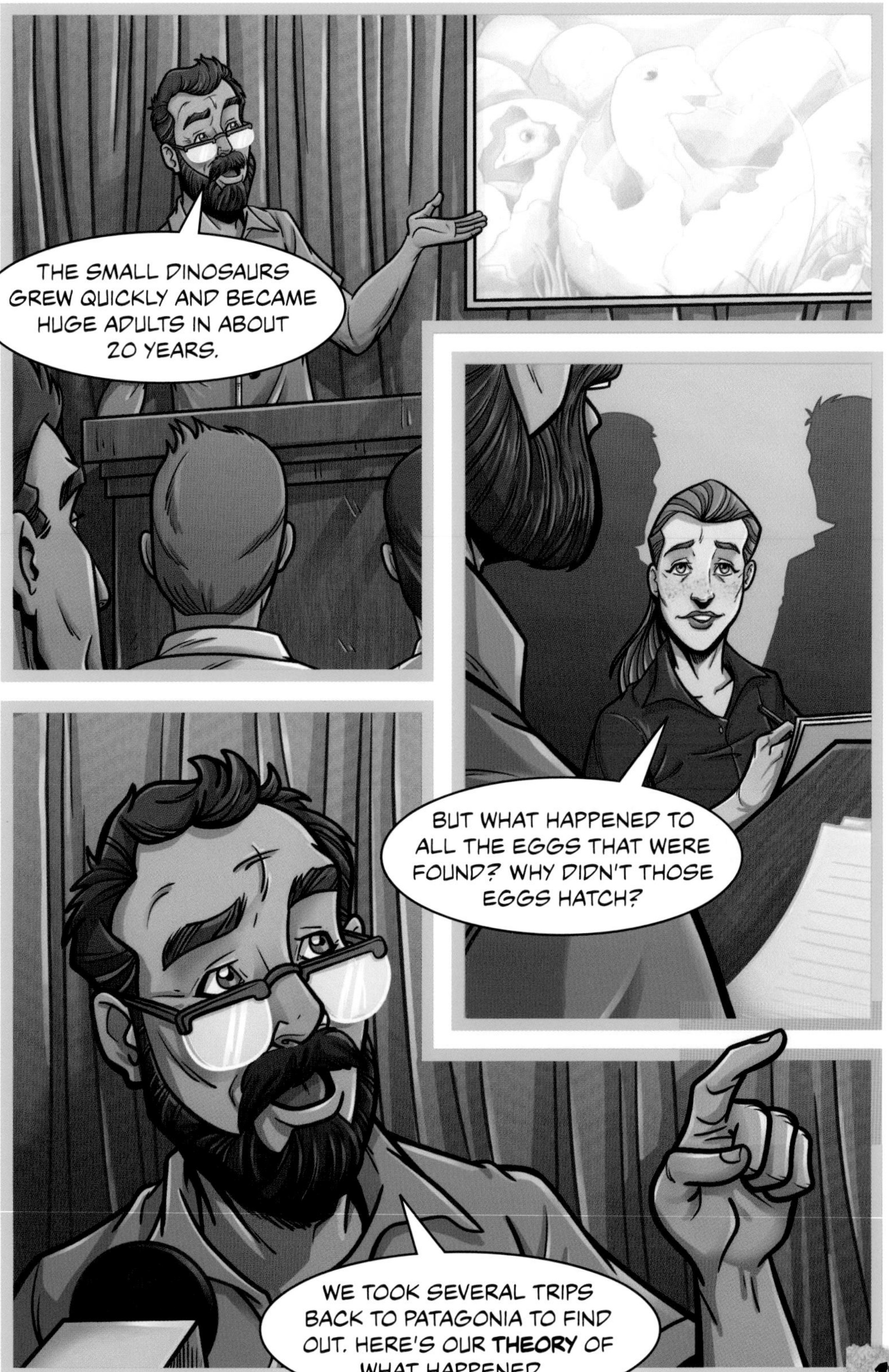
THE SMALL DINOSAURS GREW QUICKLY AND BECAME HUGE ADULTS IN ABOUT 20 YEARS.
BUT WHAT HAPPENED TO ALL THE EGGS THAT WERE FOUND? WHY DIDN'T THOSE EGGS HATCH?
WE TOOK SEVERAL TRIPS BACK TO PATAGONIA TO FIND OUT. HERE'S OUR **THEORY** OF WHAT HAPPENED...

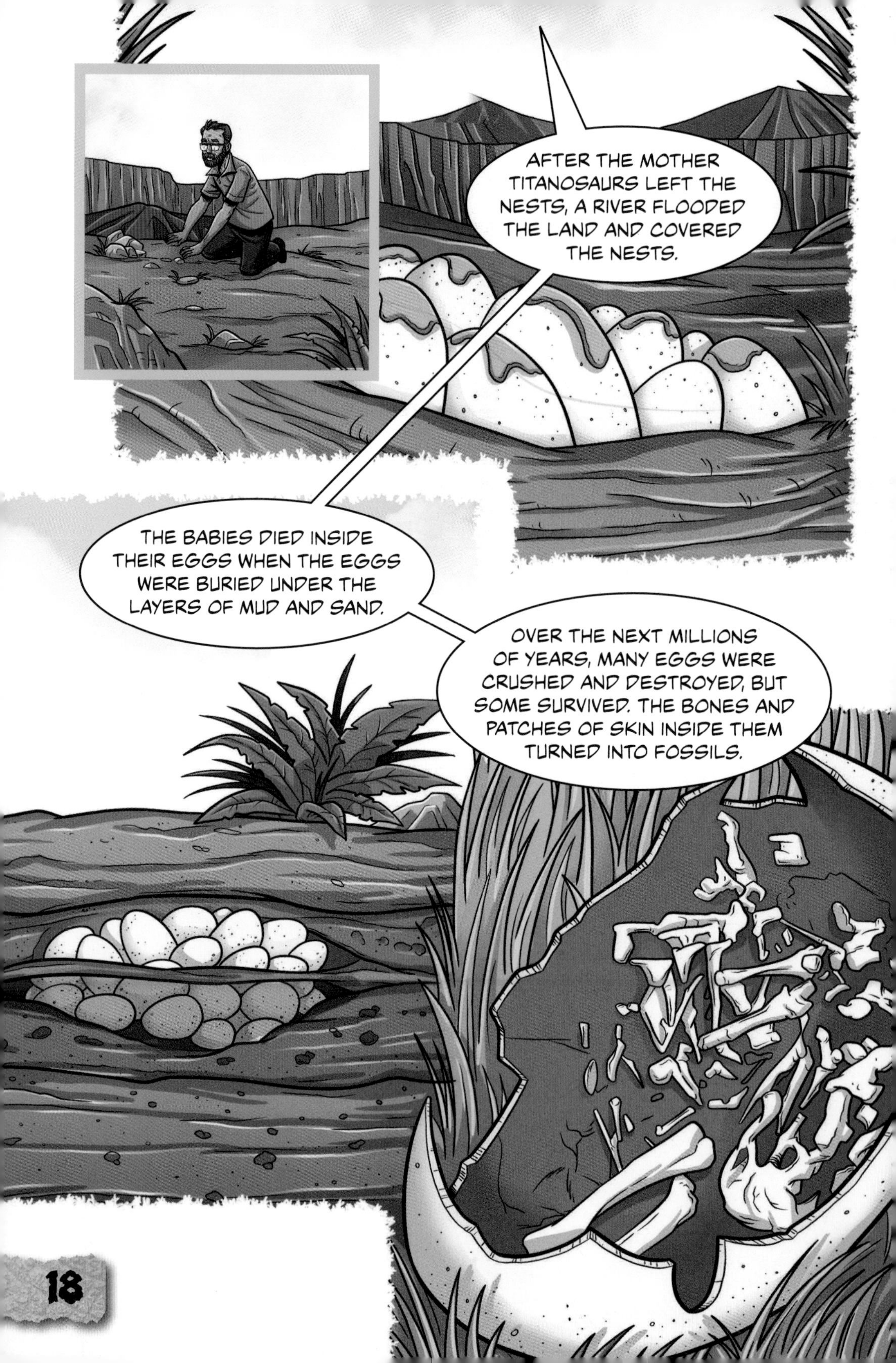
AFTER THE MOTHER TITANOSAURS LEFT THE NESTS, A RIVER FLOODED THE LAND AND COVERED THE NESTS.
THE BABIES DIED INSIDE THEIR EGGS WHEN THE EGGS WERE BURIED UNDER THE LAYERS OF MUD AND SAND.
OVER THE NEXT MILLIONS OF YEARS, MANY EGGS WERE CRUSHED AND DESTROYED, BUT SOME SURVIVED. THE BONES AND PATCHES OF SKIN INSIDE THEM TURNED INTO FOSSILS.

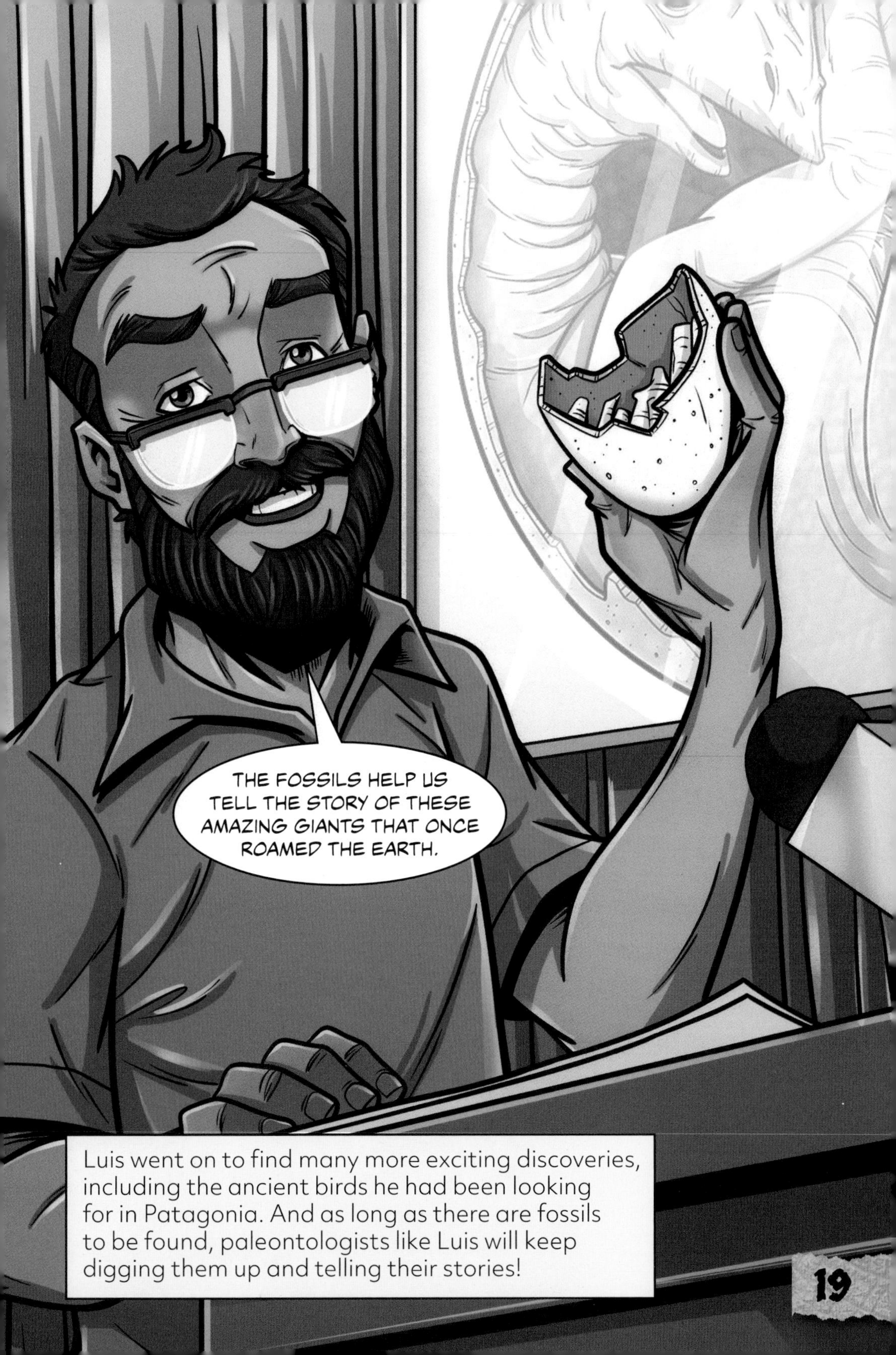
THE FOSSILS HELP US TELL THE STORY OF THESE AMAZING GIANTS THAT ONCE ROAMED THE EARTH.
Luis went on to find many more exciting discoveries, including the ancient birds he had been looking for in Patagonia. And as long as there are fossils to be found, paleontologists like Luis will keep digging them up and telling their stories!

Who Lived with the Titanosaurs?

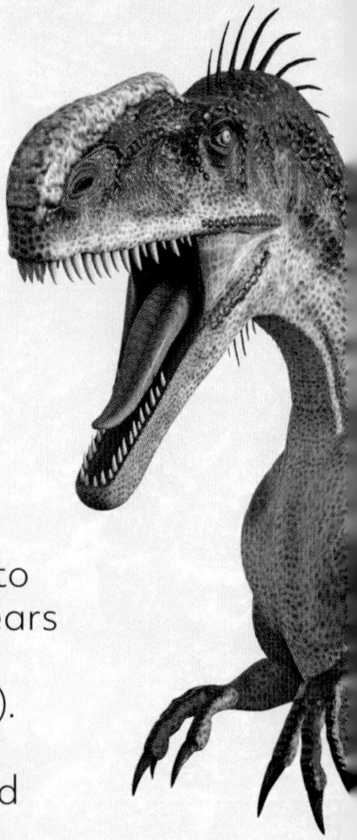

Dinosaurs lived on Earth for around 150 million years. Scientists divide the time in which the dinosaurs lived into three periods—the Triassic period (252 to 201 million years ago), the Jurassic period (201 to 145 million years ago), and the Cretaceous period (145 to 66 million years ago).

The titanosaurs that Luis Chiappe found inside fossilized eggs lived near the end of the Cretaceous period. Here are three dinosaurs that lived at the same time and in the same places as the titanosaurs.

CARNOTAURUS (*kar*-noh-TOR-uhss)

This fierce meat-eater hunted titanosaurs—probably by targeting the younger and smaller animals. What else do we know about *Carnotaurus*?

- It was smaller than the titanosaurs.
- It had long, powerful back legs and tiny arms.
- It had rows of pointy bumps running down its rough skin.
- It was 25 ft (7.6 m) long.

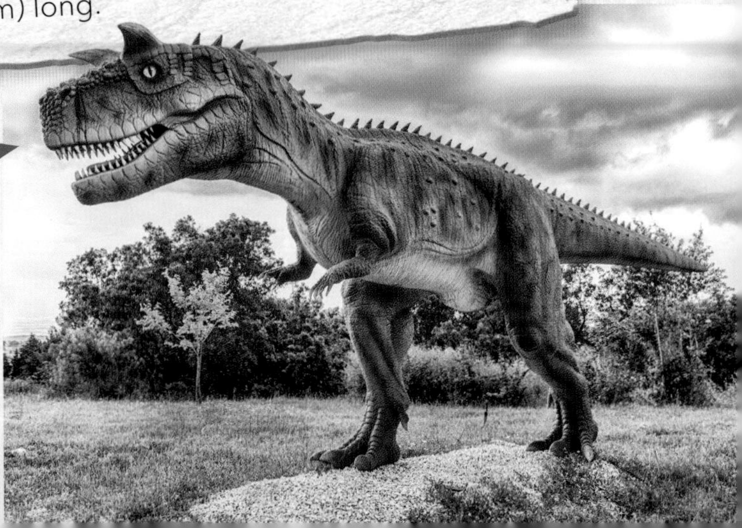

AUCASAURUS

(ow-kuh-SOR-uhss)

This smaller relative of *Carnotaurus* was discovered by Luis's team. Like *Carnotaurus*, it ate titanosaurs. What have we learned about *Aucasaurus*?

- It had small horns on its head.
- It had razor-sharp claws on its powerful legs.
- It was 20 ft (6 m) long.

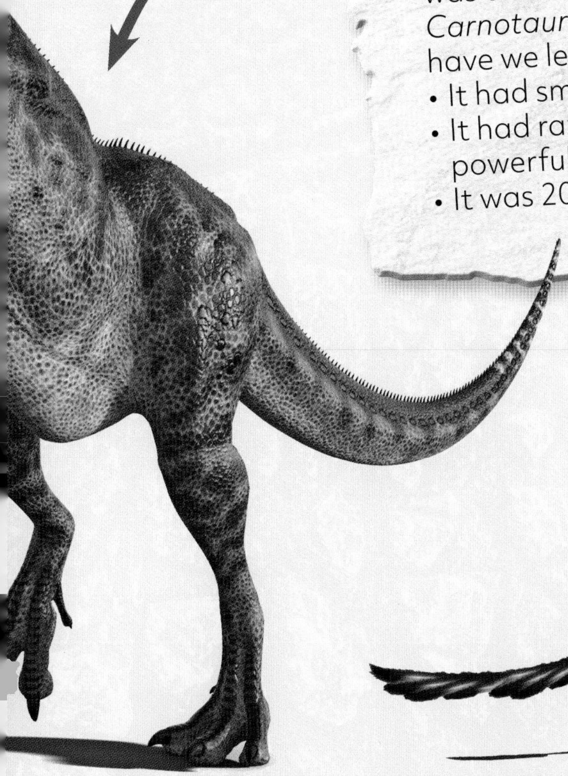

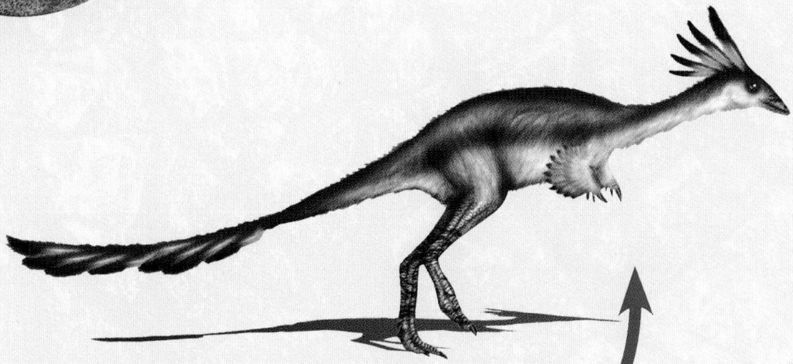

ALVAREZSAURUS

(*al*-vuh-rez-SOR-uhss)

This meat-eater lived side-by-side with the titanosaurs. Yet it was far too small to hunt them. Instead, it used its powerful thumbs to tear apart tree bark and eat the bugs that it found. What was the *Alvarezsaurus* like?

- It had a long tail, short arms, and long legs.
- It could probably run fast.
- It was 4 ft (1.2 m) long.

What Is Paleontology?

Paleontology is the study of fossils, which are what is left of things that lived millions of years ago. Fossils are found in rock. Paleontologists use special tools to carefully remove the fossils from the rock so they can study them. By studying fossils, paleontologists can figure out where a plant or animal lived, what it looked like, and how it lived.

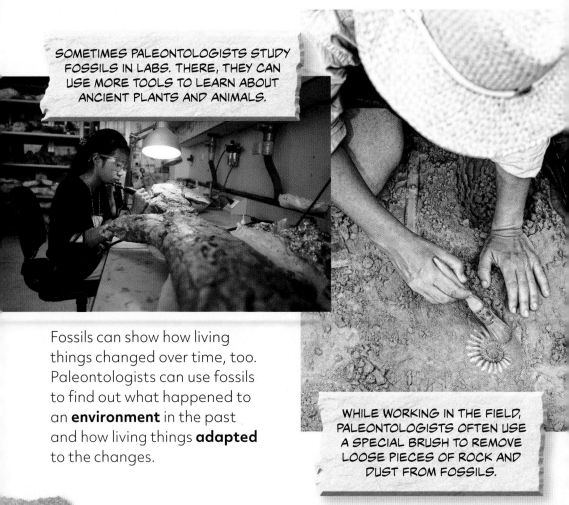

SOMETIMES PALEONTOLOGISTS STUDY FOSSILS IN LABS. THERE, THEY CAN USE MORE TOOLS TO LEARN ABOUT ANCIENT PLANTS AND ANIMALS.

Fossils can show how living things changed over time, too. Paleontologists can use fossils to find out what happened to an **environment** in the past and how living things **adapted** to the changes.

WHILE WORKING IN THE FIELD, PALEONTOLOGISTS OFTEN USE A SPECIAL BRUSH TO REMOVE LOOSE PIECES OF ROCK AND DUST FROM FOSSILS.

Glossary

adapted changed in order to handle new conditions

ancient very old

environment the conditions that surround a living thing

evidence proof of something

fossilized turned into a fossil

fossils the hardened remains of things that lived long ago

hatched emerged from its egg

laboratory a place in which scientists study

nesting site an area in which animals lay eggs

paleontologist a scientist who studies fossils to find out about life in the past

unhatched not yet emerged from an egg

theory an idea that trys to explain something

FOSSILS HELP SCIENTISTS UNDERSTAND WHAT DINOSAURS LOOKED LIKE. THEY CAN USE THIS INFORMATION TO BUILD MODELS OF THEM.

Index

Read More

Hibbert, Clare. *Giant Dinosaurs: Sauropods (Dino Explorers).* New York: Enslow Publishing, 2019.

Hirsch, Rebecca E. *Diplodocus (Finding Dinosaurs).* Lake Elmo, MN: Focus Readers, 2018.

Woodward, John. *Dinosaur! Dinosaurs and Other Amazing Prehistoric Creatures as You've Never Seen Them Before.* New York: DK Publishing, 2019.

Learn More Online

1. Go to **www.factsurfer.com** or scan the QR code below.
2. Enter "**Tiny Giants**" into the search box.
3. Click on the cover of this book to see a list of websites.